C0046 00935

D0313467

World Tales

# Baba Yaga

ıpı
54 Clar
Glasgo
Phor

This boo
be rene
date, au

A Russian tale told by Martin Waddell

Illustrated by David Lopez

W
FRANKLIN WATTS
LONDON•SYDNEY

First published in 2009 by
Franklin Watts
338 Euston Road
London
NW1 3BH

Franklin Watts Australia
Level 17/207 Kent Street
Sydney
NSW 2000

Text © Martin Waddell 2009
Illustration © David Lopez 2009

The rights of Martin Waddell to be identified as the author and David Lopez as the illustrator of this Work have been asserted in accordance with the Copyright, Designs and Patents Act, 1988.

All rights reserved. No part of this publication may be reproduced, stored in a retrieval system, or transmitted in any form or by any means, electronic, mechanical, photocopy, recording or otherwise, without the prior written permission of the copyright owner.

A CIP catalogue record for this book is available from the British Library.

ISBN 978 0 7496 8594 2 (hbk)
ISBN 978 0 7496 8600 0 (pbk)

**Series Editor:** Jackie Hamley
**Series Advisor:** Dr Barrie Wade
**Series Designer:** Peter Scoulding

Printed in China

Franklin Watts is a division of
Hachette Children's Books,
an Hachette UK company.
www.hachette.co.uk

This tale comes from Russia. Can you find Russia on a map?

GLASGOW CITY COUNCIL
LIBRARIES INFORMATION & LEARNING

| C004600935 | |
|---|---|
| C | PETERS |
| 16-Aug-2010 | £3.99 |
| JF | |

Once there was a mean witch called Baba Yaga.

She lived in a magic hut that walked about on two legs like a hen. A girl called Anya came to the hut.

Anya heard a cat crying and a dog whining miserably. She opened the creaky front door.

Anya fed the cat ...

gave the thin

dog a bone ...

and put oil on the

rusty door hinges.

Then Baba Yaga caught Anya.

"Dinner!" Baba Yaga said, smacking her lips.

"Warn me if my dinner tries to escape!" Baba Yaga told her cat.

The cat hissed and showed Anya her claws. But ...

... the cat came to Anya when Baba Yaga had gone. "You fed me, so I will help you escape. You were kinder to me than Baba Yaga ever was," it purred.

"I know you won't squeak and warn Baba Yaga!" the cat told the door.

"Anya was kind to you and oiled your hinges."

The door opened without a sound.

BABA YAGA

"I know you won't bark
and warn Baba Yaga!"
the cat told the dog.

"Anya was kind to you and gave you a bone."

The dog wagged his tail and let Anya pass.

**"Who let my dinner escape?"**

howled Baba Yaga.

The cat looked at the sky.
The dog stared up a tree.

The door slowly opened and shut, without a creak.

# And Baba Yaga ...

# ... got no dinner!

# Puzzle 1

Put these pictures in the correct order.
Now tell the story in your own words.
What different endings can you think of?

# Puzzle 2

kind gentle
frightening

scary horrid
generous

wicked nasty
helpful

Choose the correct adjectives for each character. Which adjectives are incorrect? Turn over to find the answers.

# Answers

## Puzzle 1

The correct order is: 1c, 2e, 3f, 4b, 5d, 6a

## Puzzle 2

**Anya**: the correct adjectives are gentle, kind

The incorrect adjective is frightening

**Baba Yaga**: the correct adjectives are horrid, scary

The incorrect adjective is generous

**The cat**: the correct adjective is helpful

The incorrect adjectives are nasty, wicked


## Look out for Leapfrog fairy tales:

**Cinderella**
ISBN 978 0 7496 4228 0

**The Three Little Pigs**
ISBN 978 0 7496 4227 3

**Jack and the Beanstalk**
ISBN 978 0 7496 4229 7

**The Three Billy Goats Gruff**
ISBN 978 0 7496 4226 6

**Goldilocks and the Three Bears**
ISBN 978 0 7496 4225 9

**Little Red Riding Hood**
ISBN 978 0 7496 4224 2

**Rapunzel**
ISBN 978 0 7496 6159 5

**Snow White**
ISBN 978 0 7496 6161 8

**The Emperor's New Clothes**
ISBN 978 0 7496 6163 2

**The Pied Piper of Hamelin**
ISBN 978 0 7496 6164 9

**Hansel and Gretel**
ISBN 978 0 7496 6162 5

**The Sleeping Beauty**
ISBN 978 0 7496 6160 1

**Rumpelstiltskin**
ISBN 978 0 7496 6165 6

**The Ugly Duckling**
ISBN 978 0 7496 6166 3

**Puss in Boots**
ISBN 978 0 7496 6167 0

**The Frog Prince**
ISBN 978 0 7496 6168 7

**The Princess and the Pea**
ISBN 978 0 7496 6169 4

**Dick Whittington**
ISBN 978 0 7496 6170 0

**The Little Match Girl**
ISBN 978 0 7496 6582 1

**The Elves and the Shoemaker**
ISBN 978 0 7496 6581 4

**The Little Mermaid**
ISBN 978 0 7496 6583 8

**The Little Red Hen**
ISBN 978 0 7496 6585 2

**The Nightingale**
ISBN 978 0 7496 6586 9

**Thumbelina**
ISBN 978 0 7496 6587 6

**For more Leapfrog books go to:** www.franklinwatts.co.uk